Stone Window

Ann Robinson

To Rhoda –
Many thanks
to helping me on my
path – Enjoy –
Love,
Anne

Stone Window

Ann Robinson

Bark for Me

狗

Publications

Fairfax, California
2014

Bark for Me

狗

Publications

To the memory of

Edith Robinson who still walks among us,

and to Peggy, Jerry, Sara, Joe & Jack

Acknowledgments

Grateful acknowledgment is made to the editors of the journals and anthologies who first published the following poems. The poems, sometimes in earlier versions, appeared as follows:

Amarillo Bay: "Red Queen," "Limbo"
American Literary Review: "Riding the Train at Fifteen"
Chaffin Journal: "Fire"
Coe Review: "Dutchman's Pipe"
Compass Rose: "December Paradise"
Connecticut Review: "31 Boulevard Terrace"
Diner: "After Lorca"
Diverse Voices Quarterly: "Falling in Love with a Stranger Across the Street"
Eclipse: "His Daughter"
Forge: "Where Are All Those Grade B Actresses?"
Fourteen Hills: "The Crossing"
Hiram Poetry Review: "Counting Hoops"
Marin Poetry Center Anthology: "Gospel"
Natural Bridge: "The Baptism"
Passager: "Lorca in New York City"
Poet Lore: "1957: Central High School"
RiverSedge: "First"
Schuykill Valley Journal of the Arts: "Stone Window"
Spoon River Review: "Lark Song," "Marriage"
Valparaiso Poetry Review: "New York Train Station"
Weave Magazine: "Northwest Wolves"
Whiskey Island Magazine: "The Old Woman in the Shoe"
Zone 3: "Fire Dance"

Many thanks to Barbara S. Brauer, Kate Peper, Tom Centolella, Ella Eytan, Phyllis Teplitz, Molly Fisk, Jane Miller, Raffi D'Bourgo, and a special thanks to April Ossmann, Joe Zaccardi and Rose Black, for the curved patience of saints.

Also, my gratitude to the editors of the *Marin Poetry Center Anthology* for nominating my poem "Gospel" for a Pushcart prize.

Contents

III

I

Stone Window

His uniform, medals,
like false stars
fall across the floor.

Close your eyes,
he commands.

The walls become a halo.
The child's eyes, a stolen river.

Her school satchel
propped against his boot
in shadow.
Every window turned to stone.

In the nearby village,
her mother waits at the door,
a shawl of candles on the mantel.

The trees have turned white this year,
always it will be the last time.

31 Boulevard Terrace

The father and son argue on the lawn tonight.
John pounds his Chevy's hood,
pulse quick like an alibi.

His father hits their elm with a wooden bat,
two halves broken into two angry truths.

Neighbors wait in doorways,
frozen under porchlight.

Days, the father broods and drinks;
John, dark and thin
as a burned needle.

They forget the house
they built together—roof already
pockmarked by rain,
twenty-five guns in the garage
as a hobby.

Next door, I stand with my back flat against
the bedroom wall,
memorizing my body's outline
in the mirror,
my white and blueness.

Five years I have slept in each room
too close to loaded guns,
any notion of family
picked clean by rage,

my fence shifting
and separating until only
the rubble-covered ground remains.

The Baptism

We stood waist deep in the river:
The women in long white gowns,
the men with their Sunday suits.
Our children called us half people
until they became the same.
We didn't so much enter the water
as fall into the light, the sun
almost white above the blue ridge,
and the water broke and broke,
children floating in bright clothing
twirled like little parachutes
as each of us walked in to be re-born.

Maybe I'm telling you this
because I enjoy the lie.
Some never entered the water, clinging
to shore like apparitions.
The rest of us were pushed under
with a force that tore at any roots.
We could see the bitten-off sun,
the wavering moon arrive.
We learned to breathe
as the living breathed.
We thought we would never surface again.

Jerry Lee

Take Sun Studio lit by booze
and bright capsules,
Jerry at the piano,
his swivel and spit.

Married his thirteen-year-old cousin,
house paid, Christmas lights year around,
more clothes than she could wear.
She left him, grew an inch taller.

His third wife drowned in a swimming pool after an argument.
I ain't sinned, he said at the inquest.

Jerry Lee pounded the piano keys
like a knife cleaving light.

He broke thirty metronomes
and never sat down.

Sang *Whole Lotta Shakin',*
as if he had lived it,
as if he'd show us how.

After the Storm

Someone was writing me from candlelight.
I saw his curled shadow in the second storey
window, propped a ladder against the wall

and climbed. I waited in his light
while he wrote and revised me,
made me climb down the ladder.

Now he writes how the night lanterns me,
how my beauty is taller than the ladder
he makes me climb again.

The night once cold, now
so hot, I flush and sweat.
Now he's written me naked,
my flesh pearls and goose-bumps.

Why would he write me in such a way?
Open me like a book,
exposing the words inside.
Close the window on my hands.

December Paradise

My mother was two people when she drank.
Mauve silk and vodka,
caressing everyone and spilling herself on carpets.

Hours later, the thinnest of shrieks,
complaining nothing was right.

Saturdays, she quieted by degrees,
wondering about the continual snows
through clean kitchen windows.

The snowman guarded the front yard
through the hard weather.
Coal eyes like planets, bowl belly, a shield.

I could see the strangers' faces
as I stood small behind his snow body.
I threw snowballs, each larger than the last.

Sometimes my mother stood in the doorway
without her familiar glass,

hands trembling for something to hold,
against the sum of all that whiteness.

Red Queen

Marie Antoinette played her
and lost her life.
Dryden spilled ale on her.

Shakespeare folded her into Desdemona.
Alice banished her down a well of loneliness.

The Red Queen longed for escape,
tired of being played, her colors rubbing off.
Outside, the sounds of children.

While her lover, the Knave,
slept with odd numbers,
she heard children calling,
dreamed of open windows,
of sunshine seizing her, escape
to the bird-filled trees.

Freedom in a wilderness.
The Queen grim in solitude.
The grass smelled sharp enough
to cut her, the roses, a royal
flush.

New York Train Station

From the commuter window,
stars burn blue holes in a bluer
firmament, a map my veined hand
mirrors.

The train stops and starts,
punctuated by my arrhythmia.

Doomed to travel
without arriving, till small, oval faces click
into view under the platform's dim lights,
trench coats, boots, the ambivalent stares.

Their apartments could be mine.
I will stand on any step and knock.
A door swings open,
the heavenly music surprises me.
I enter without being invited.

The Indefinite

Maybe I can't forget
the morning he left,
the willow in shade
by my closed window.
Each branch sounding
a note of what was missing,
the finch without song.

Try to start a line
with passion,
the first word
before Eden or dreams.

Like a lyric refrain,
ode to the unpeopled streets.

I pretend he waits in the empty
apartment next door.

You've got such young hands,
I used to tell him,
impression of bone and sinew,
what carries us.

Ode to an Exclamation Point

You meet me at the bar, a little late
but you quicken my slur.
You stand on a beat-up barstool,
your vertical arrow ending each sentence,
and yes, after six drinks,
I am in love with your wild hair, short feet,
your impatience with the middle of anything.
You leap ahead of my sentences,
give me some fizz,
ending my story of a burning house, saved
infants and cats,
and me not even a fireman.
You stay with me, loyal dart,
artful string, you stalk me like a lover—
because of you, I view myself as astonishment,
because of you I don't close my eyes.

Marriage

Martha's at the sink,
washing crystal.

The thirty-dollar
anniversary goblet
shatters, but fractures
delight her.
She arranges shards
like puzzle pieces
on the dinner table.

Latex gloves
drown each china plate.
Her husband's at the back door
of their neighbor,
tips his lover's face up.
His mouth seizes hers.
The yellow bulb
captures a stanza,
her hips slide and catch.

She's the divorced female
with a swimming pool
wears a bathing suit
as if it were her only clothing.

Tonight is Martha's night.
She arranges broken glass
on the table,
splintered china
on the chairs.
Everything has to be clean.

Where Are All Those Grade B Movie Actresses?

Her real name is Rita Piceno, mid-forties,
skin peeling from too much makeup.
She goes home in tennis shoes to a one-room apartment.

People recognize her, but can't recall from where,
though when her leading man signed autographs,
he always mentioned her name.

Her three-way mirror knows best.
I am your honey lips, your lady bell,
shot forty-three times, divorced fifteen, lost custody
of thirty-two children, murdered twelve husbands;
she couldn't memorize,
her lines were taped on walls.

Hung from a shower curtain, slept with thirty men,
although cameras shot only an empty bed.
She acted pathos so many times
she no longer feels,
and can't imagine herself ten years from now.

In her next movie, her chandelier earrings
will be lost in the backseat
of Lee Marvin's convertible,
as the car stalls on a cliff:

I am your big blonde baby, your one and only, aren't I?
Platinum hair framing her practiced pout.

Northwest Wolves

Know me by my final call,
heart stopped by a rifle shot.
Hung by my hind legs,
left to freeze.
My fur, crystalline grey, moon-blurred,
darker where I bled.

Swinging in a hard wind,
I no longer want or need,
my face thin with ice.

Ain't you a beauty,
sighed the hunter,

my eyes keen with ghosts,
what the snow has made.

First Knowledge

Why didn't I just stay
in the loft, sweet with hay,

with John's strong,
unscarred hands on me.

When he asked for a smile,
drew a straw across my lips,

I saw what would happen,
how my body would break
over plowing earth,

the sound of combines
entering every room, so I learned
to hate silence, too, the big emptiness,

even for one night, but wasn't it always so?

Dutchman's Pipe

What scent drove this creature
into the wrong hour?

The fly circled the piped flower's rim,
wandered into the fluted portals.

This heart-shaped flower
resting on a vine,

small trap
of loveliness.

The fly returned
to my many-petalled city,
drunk with pain,
dying on the flagstone.

In my garden,
beauty is dangerous.

Pollen stings, a bee warns,
my wrists cinched by vines.

I confine myself here,
doubtful of expectations.
I see how the hummingbird
outpaces its heart.

Falling in Love with a Stranger Across the Street

Not a million red lights
could stop me from loving you.

Tall in leather, cobalt tough and handsome.
On the street of just me and you,
yearning's a yanked string.

I take off my coat,
and this dress, bruised with years.
I turned into spangled silk.

I aimed my smile,
guessing at you.
An inner city bus

passed between us
on its last route.

Gospel

I've always been a doubter;
I live below the surface.

The spite moon stalks me
and sheds no light.

I practice saying *no*.
Never surrender.

The fig tree opens, but the fruit
is only fit for ornament.

I once believed
freedom was given

but I choose it.
The choices, the size of my hands.

I look out the chapel window
as each leaf broadens
in the working garden.

You wait there in shadows,
endless as a Sunday afternoon.

And still you do not speak to me
as if I, too, am what remains.

II

Riding the Train at Fifteen

Stranger on a train.
Asleep next to me, face fragile
as something unborn.

I took his wallet from his pocket, telling myself
I had good reason,
slipping through door after door,
and lurching aisles.

A hallway of mirrors appeared,
each passenger's whisper,
each look folded behind newspaper.

In the last car, I fumbled
through his identity, credit cards,
pictures of his family in a parade,
the baby on a spoonful of sun.

The train windows passed
through me like mist, their ghostly clouds,
tree branches like winter veins.
I could say it was divorce, or death, or a fad,

but no, it was just a state of being:
like a bird turning on itself,
or rain that won't come down.

I left his wallet on a seat, put the money
in my pocket. Spent the day
looking at myself in the mirror.
It was touching, that look,
every piece of me breaking off at once.

Lorca in New York City

A revolutionary sleeps with a gun,
a fatal edge; you cannot beg
for the past.

Lorca smoked two thousand cigarettes
to keep from writing lyrics.
He wrote speeches on mirrors, rewritten
until the glass stopped reflecting.
Bad verse piled on the rugs, windows were shut,
love was ambush.
He played jazz to his penis.
The men he loved lived in barely any light.

He went for a drive in the countryside
with a trunkful of guns, pistols.
He fired at telephone lines and wild animals
that only he would mourn.
For love, every night was last night.
Pebbles tasted like peaches. Men smelled of soot and blossoms.
The beauty of not having a god.

He built an ode at the end of a river,
her hips and breasts worthy of thirty-five lines.
He took off his vest and revolver.
His heaven had barely begun.
The margins were slender.

The Dollhouse My Father Gave Me

Gilded rooms from St. Louis,
scrolled antiques, delicacy of my father's taste.

The mother sleeps in the doll bed,
china hands folded on dreams.

The daughter in the next room,
painted eyes, her wintry face—
what becomes of porcelain?

The father in the living room,
grey-clad body leaning on the mantel,
the family clock stopped at two a.m.

The house breathes like a hidden animal,
footsteps pound the hallway,
no telling whether it's dream or beast.

Every lock guards secrets,
the mother will never awaken.

The daughter's door left half open,
the curtains pulled shut.

The dolls wait on shelves,
the hours folded in the closet.

The father waits in shadow,
what passes for love.

My Lover Is Cardboard

I cut him out,
prop him next to me,
cruise control down Rodeo Drive
in my rented Buick LeSaber.

His spunky cowboy outfit charms,
even a badge that spells, *Sheriff*.
I gave him the purloined features
of ex-lovers, both living and dead.

The unfocused eyes of La Juno's doorman,
and Lennie Caruso's hips
at the Fifth Trade Outfit.

I gave him a whopper of a penis, just
as big as Jerome Spicer's during the Ford Era.

We stroll to the Motel De Ville
in downtown Hollywood,
where the unnamed and overly named
stay, for brag rights to expensive sex.

The all-night manager shrugs
at my cut-out doll, with chaps
stiff as any erection.

I can't afford a double bed,
so I hold him in my lap and trim his hair,
scraps littering the floor
like a poor man's confetti.

A Period Speaks to a Sentence at the Café Reale

I am not a fragment of your longing
but a final reply to earth.
I suffer the repeated grief
of false endings, *mon dieu,*
my faultless gaze has made you whole.

I knew Hemingway when he lost
his language to drink and lazy bulls.
I was his conclusion.

Look at Baudelaire, no more
to me than table art.
I stopped those pretty rhymes,
I am the irrevocable ending.

No writer can live
without my black pearls.
My petite love, I will keep you
from falling or shove you over the edge.

At the Café Reale in Paris,
every fatuous sentence is astonished
at your demise.
I have written you off
and still you follow me,
like a hound to its tongue.

Southern Narrative

Everything gone wrong except for Jesus
on the rooftop of an Arkansas church,
or kneeling on moss of the Pentecostal steps.
You skid into sin and the dirty sheets
of a stranger, listening for
your grandmother's censure,

her grey eyes on *no* and *no;*
the bible on a dollied tabletop,
Jack Benny on the radio.

The past is a trick to be forgiven
or forgotten: vodka you mistook for the Holy Grail.
Stairs that descended into 18 states,

you slumped over tables at all-night diners
on a quest turned soulless.

No memory of that night you gave up God,
washed of sin as you stare mutely at the church
glowing like a Vegas without dreams.

The Old Woman in the Shoe

I can't identify what's broken,
or kiss again your shade
blue eyes, the smoky angles
of your body lost as you wandered
next door to fine leather
and tenderness.

After twenty-six children,
you forgot our names,
briefest wishes, the darkest cries.

Fifty-two hands and prayers at bedtime,
lullabies falling
on a cracked cradle,
the oldest sliding down the tongue,
the youngest tangled in laces;

forgive us, every stained surface,
carved window—greedy, smeared
faces peering out—brutal husband,

I was so in love with you
I hated my own children
enough to murder them in my mind
just to have you back again.

I think all this and not you,
the rough edges of home,
or this: love is what we survive.

Lark Song

The mad woman running
across the field wearing a raincoat,
no bad weather in sight—

sees them everywhere:
on the orange tongue of sky or filed
among tall grasses where skylarks built thin-bone nests,
the hatchlings crazy with calling—

I've got twenty children in the clouds,
she says, imitating their flight
at the alehouse, her raincoat as wings.
She tells tales of an army of larks
who sang her through two wars,

the village of Lancaster, where she swam naked
with a hundred soldiers' ghosts,
lifting into starlight, her long limbs freed at last
from this mocking earth
to a thousand whistles, the exultation of multitudes.

The Crossing

The air blackens and someone whispers,
The devil is among us. The fans click on and off
in the transport truck

and walls strain with heat. The tropic pulse
is not the body's but the clay earth we came from.

Nothing is imagined, not the sound
of an engine idling or boots striking gravel.

The yellow eyes of the border patrol as the door slides open.
Instinct blinds us
as we run into the August night,

gunfire following and I duck into the arid landscape,
become the tallest of trees, moon along the sides,
seeing the brief lives along the road.

A man cradles what's left of him, a woman simply folds.
The only sound was a long time ago.

I almost cannot believe it—a child tries to fly
among these leaves.

Mason Jar

We leave the clatter of forks and knives,
turn off the kitchen light to see the fireflies
flit within glass on the window sill.
We are happy as only country children can be.

But even houses have doubts,
wary of their residents.
The truck drove into the backyard
years ago, a gun on a rack,
dead animals in the back.

We let the fireflies out,
but they followed our running
through the yard and field.

Our paths were hidden
among whippoorwill, brush,
and whatever calls back.
Moonlight consoled some of us,
at least the ones who made it.

First

A field of cardinals
bloomed in my Nikon
in three snapshots.

Cornfields beside them and sky,
a chorus of yellows, blues.
The birds abandoned
the field, the silence
like a derisive
whisper behind a wall.

I never liked the ending of anything.
I never liked how people closed doors
or left the front porch
steps to say goodbye.

Seeing the flock of birds,
I saw I'd never lived.

The radiance of what is missing,
like those scattered stalks in snapshot
twenty-three, now cut and scattered,
and the birds, those radiant creatures,
where are they now?

Execution

A blade comes down,
the scaffold tears,
the long stairs break.

That winter the trees wore ice.
Lights glinting off branches
drew diagrams for me.

I saw my bones where muscles
should be,
my hair styled by sleet.

I threw a white tantrum
but no one cared,
I plotted escape, flight
through freezing sky.

Each atom of me understood
space and no one.

First father, then Mother,
entered my bitter room.
Father brushed my hair

until each strand fell out.
Mother sold my hair to a vendor.
Grandmother framed my naked head
against the snow outside my window.

My body prepared for terror.
I was made to climb stairs, blindfolded,
made to touch myself like a bride.

The scaffold smelled like lavender.
I wore a black cap and memory.

Living with the Enemy

At the point of departure, the galaxy tears.

To stay, you must be

a windup toy, used or useless;

after his knife hit your shoulder,

you knelt in silver. Orion's white belt

thrown down, hear the celestial clamor,

see the puncture where God has been—

when you look up, the eclipse begins.

San Joaquin Wildlife Refuge

A single gunshot, sky folded into wings,
sheets of snow geese
and ibis, ink drops in clouds.

The Sandhill cranes never moved.
The wood ducks imitated a painting.
I envied their calm.

At the refuge, I slept for a week
in my car, jacked on caffeine and donuts.
Bundled in woolens at night, not a hunter
but a bum.

I lost my job, my watch,
I don't know the hour
of my return. The tiny camera that shot

the moment into immortality—out of film.
I'm inventing a lexicon
for impermanence.

The white-tailed kite over sedge
never returns, the red shouldered hawk,
dropped by a bullet.

The no trespassing sign
vanishes when I enter.

When I see flocks among cattails
and road signs,
I am less lonely, a language
that never completes itself.

His Daughter

In a third grade play,
she was a hydrangea,
a devastation of petals.
At sixteen she stalked the malls,
a caricature of breasts,
the eyes fringed as a pansy.

She became a stranger
who lived in a room
with potato chips, loose soil,
headphones wrapped
around un-watered plants.

When the boys arrived,
her father thought of stamen,
pistils, himself at that age,
full of thrust and yearning,
sap flowing under brush
and the knowledge
that nothing is forgiven.

He imagined her, helpless
of course, in backseats.
An orchid folding
under someone's breath,
the moon breaking into seeds.

At the Orchid Pavilion

The hothouse ones inveigle you
through their soft portals
to an empty chamber.

No comfort to be had here,
only the pronged tongue,
the haughty cup.

Still, you stare at those African colors,
as if they could talk to you.

Simply to breathe their air
puts them to death
or so the vendor says—
you pause at that shadow.

Last night, you traced
the fragile spots of your body,
dim openings of childhood—
the way he sauntered into a room,
the scars on your wrists.

Thwarting your desire
is their beauty and loss.

You step closer to those empty flowers—
the vendor says *stop,*
and you do.

Limbo

After several weeks, I quit searching
the ravine behind my house,
the brambles and cicada trails,
the creek leading to my working neighbors
and late afternoon silence.

I searched shelters,
animals in cages, the size of dreams and wishes,
not unlike my cat who lived
as I did, in spurts of joy and depression.

I learned the meaning of solitude,
of what I could not hold.

Each window in my house, unlit,
as if someone had moved away,

I imagine the place my cat is tonight,
listening for me as I listen for him,
treading the stone edges, rattling
the dark.

Counting Hoops

The boy across the street plays
basketball at midnight.
Through the hooped moon
the ball rises, dips
into the net.

Such a small boy,
such a tightfisted moon.
His father dying
in a wheelchair by the window.

His mother asleep on the couch,
the TV light bluing the window.

The boy racks up points.
I will not yell out my window—
three months of this incessant pounding,
my fingers trembling
around coffee cups.
I've begun to memorize patterns,
hating sounds that dip
and dribble; I sleep to the pulse
of his scores and misses.

This morning a vast absence
of sound, the lights all off, cars gone.
In the brief seconds after dreams,
when I didn't know where I was,
I knew a difference.

III

Leda in the City

Even that lovely face wasn't immune
to the swan's white gaze.

His eyes shone cool as the moon
and through that coarse light she saw cities rise
and fall, and the dead follow her children.

His wings unfolded her arms and legs,
her city clothes dropped over rooftops.

The weather was Mercury's, all tirades and appeals.
No heavens moved for her and she clung
to the notion that force was necessary for myth.

How gods expand on themselves
and abandon you at high altitudes.

The bird left her on an eleventh floor roof
in the midst of the polluted city,
wings slightly parted, as he transformed.

She described it to everyone at the party,
sipping a cocktail, lovely in silk.
But no one believed her,

they wanted photographs,
proof of magic.

Though she remembered desiring much,
she believed in very little, until her mirror
reflected her as a bird, a darker one,

whose eyes told her of offspring who would
murder, rape and pillage
in the name of love.

Firewater

I didn't want to go home,
because I knew you'd be there,

behind the broken tree in the front yard,
lightless windowpanes,

even horses, with their brave syntax,
and wild running, remind me of your rants.

You're here again,
sitting in the floral chair.
Upstaged, bald, the old runner,
track star with no remembrance of the past.

You walked three miles from the grave
to tell me memory is whiskey
raining from your mind's sky,
your teeth cracking ice.

One midnight in Texas,
you hit my seven-year-old head
because you didn't like questions.

The floor breaks open, to no road,
the void returning, the engine shaking
against the ribcage, you
slumped drunk on the wheel,

four visits to your grave last week
and still the car won't stop.

Electra Speaks

I was a gatherer of signs and portents,
and gifts, elusive like comets.
Snakes in chairs told fortunes

and the city was wild for my tarots.
You may ask the point of seeing
the future in a deck.
The dead man always sings,

yet my mother was the one
who foretold my destinations,
tucking fishbones under my pillow.

Family is a ruse,
no one pretends for you.
All history lies under my mother's breast.

Greece's light flashes like a sword
as I stand on a shambling hill.
Tonight, we are the only gods.

Nightmare

I couldn't sleep.
I turned on the TV from the big living room chair.
My mother and father
talking to me from the blue screen.
Ten years since they died.
The darkness shaking,
the volume so low
it sounded like a draft.
They explained how and why
my life turned rotten.
My hearing exclusive of *should*
and *don't*.
My vision, a tunnel.
I left the room while they droned on.
An owl called outside, the extinct kind.

What We See

In every imagination
a semblance of truth:
great egrets bring the mind back to angels,

how light erases a shadow here, a dot there,
till you no longer know what you see;

the beach where the angels march disappears,
caught in the center of the eye—
something fleeing.

Just as the mistake of lines and light
erases reality: his tough hands,

sun-burned arms,
blown kiss almost muscular—

The line breaks here,
what moves through and around you, treacherous.

The way he touches with or without love
and you can't stop wanting.

But what happens
is imagination, nothing better.
I prefer to be loved by a word,
than this familiar emptiness.

In a Bolinas Pasture

Let nature take care of itself,
the cowboy said.

The calf on its side for hours,
mouth suckling dirt.
Its fetal, dark hide drying.

The mother abandoned it
in north pasture among sage
and barb-wire.
Grieving its
misshapen head.

With binoculars, I watched
in one hundred-degree heat.

Turkey vultures stretched on posts,
red-shouldered hawks circled.

I put the binoculars in my pack,
startling at the zipper's raw sound,
the closure in my hands.

Having no children of my own,
I took a last look, the smallness of its body,
and hurried on.

Living Among the Gods

Persephone descends,
fishnet stockings
and wildflowers in her belt.

Fragile and white as a teacup,
she can't bear touching.

It wasn't consensual sex,
but she made no sound.

In the underworld, choices
were granted in smoky rooms.

The gods drank, played poker,
and shared cigars, her husband
uncommonly hairy.

Ascending once again, she wanders
the parking lot of the Orpheum,
following her image on shiny fenders.

Her dress, the wildflowers,
and here, her stockings stolen from dead bodies.

She raises one bruised arm
while cars honk and radios blare.

It's her season to return,
but the music playing in the coliseum lures her.

The violins' and trumpets' urging
enough to keep her in this asphalt world,
along with its strange noise and ungodly freedom.

1957: Central High School

September and piano lessons—
each week, I would never return.

Ten blocks away,
Federal troops held bayonets
an octave above violence.
Nine black teenagers
growing darker
against a white schoolyard.

Books like sheet music
falling on concrete,
broken chords.
The piano's metronome quickened.

Governor Orval Faubus
wore a white shirt
with rolled-up sleeves,
held a megaphone
at his Buick's side,
chanting *segregation.*

I learned *Blue Danube*
during ten days of riots.

Jazz played in North Little Rock
at the Duke Club,
where my mother's maid sang scat.

I listened through my hands
until I could no longer
feel the difference
or name it.

Solitaire

The King of Hearts comes next.
He's the unlucky one
according to the gossip of the towers.

The Queen is upstairs
with the Knave,
red curtains drawn.

The deck is thick with secrets.
Hearts bitter in their royal throats,
as the Queen later lies on her King.

The royal couple's children,
club-footed, erratic,
hidden in shuffles, rumored illegitimate,
plot against their sleeping parents.

Who shall fall from the deck
in this odd hour?

Wind troubles the turrets,
the footman sleeps in his carriage,
dogs snore on stone floors.

Here sneaks the Ace of Spades,
heartless and blackened by too many hands,
he knows that anonymity is power—

and to rule a deck, shuffle all you are,
draw your next card and begin
your life again.

Retired

I talk to myself so much
I sleep from boredom,
and wake under a fallen tree.
So many calling from the next world,
telling me I'm past tense.

A Civil Servant all those years,
I climbed the same stairs,
and soothed many cranky spirits.
I followed someone's polyester-covered ass.

I learned to pass through people
like winter, or maybe it's water.
My skin, an alphabet of experience
that I'm unlearning.

Now I float like a white nightgown
over communion rails,
or maybe commuter rails.
I see earth as a celestial pilot,
lights on a runway that never ends.

Fire Dance

Mary, the lyric one, told us
she had first-stage Alzheimer's.

The problem's to get to a bus,
poems lost, rent check
found in the trash bin.

We told her days hide
behind days for all of us.
Her poetry was still good,
lines like an unnamed flower opening,

reminds me of the way she touched
her face, over and over—

hands of forgetfulness,
hands that dropped and lost
locks and keys.

The clocks that lost time,
the waiting. Her apartment
on Divisadero, a street
she couldn't find.

When I took her to the Bart station,
she grabbed my hand,
but looked away.
Days later, I lost a wallet at work,

in line at the bank—I stood quite still.
It was enough simply to be alive.

Macular Degeneration

Front range gone,
a blur on the road
day and night.
I recognize the world
as something I used to know.
Reaching for the familiar,
the fabulous gone.

My eyes, all shadows.
The curtains drawn.
I wish for something to jolt even prayers.

Because I once saw like this:
looking behind everyone,
as if more importance
lurked there.
Not straight ahead,
not present,

and now
the sun, an opal,
blind light.

Relearning Math

The boy watched algebra unfold
on the blackboard, trying to imagine
how infinity reached past the stars.

Three miles away, his parents
were entering the Plaza Del Rey
when the bomb hit.

Sensors calibrated the explosion,
the eye closes on fiery equations
as windows were torn from panes.

The enemy was a straight line.
The boy dreamed of oceans and harbors,
his tenth grade poster of a sailor navigating blue.
You can't change time, his parents would say.

The teacher held the chalk like a threat.
How do light and sound become an equation?

At the plaza,
the two bodies held each other,
always equal to.

The boy wrote out the correct answer on the blackboard.
Without knowing why, he erased it.

Joan of Arc

Where is the soul? the clerics asked,
agreeing on the heart's smallest chamber.

They made fishnets to catch it
after the burning, but it fled
the charred body, left them holding ash.

Centuries later, we meet Joan in France.
The stake, a trimmed-down pole
set in ashes. Joan is taller
than expected, and her hair, white and long.

She uses lighter fluid on the stake,
but it will not burn, so she throws it.
It returns to her like a boomerang,
more than flesh,
less than eternity.

If you had to do it over again, we ask.
Yes, she says.
*When I looked up that day, country
surrounding me, each tree, flower, and moving cloud,
a miracle, a country beyond God.*

After Lorca

What concerns me now is a lemon,
split through the center.
A yellow basin.
The walk on both sides.
A bitter landscape,
but free to talk.

My lips intimate with it,
glad for the gift of silence,
I see better without speaking.

I follow a daily ritual,
strolling Barcelona's curving,
cobbled streets.

Strangers have followed me,
what I press to my mouth
recalls them.

Imagination is a distant soil.
I tell you all because it doesn't matter.
I have never traveled to Spain, but feel
Spain's unforgiving heat

in my backyard, among sparrows
and yucca and a lemon tree.

Ann Robinson lives in Novato, California. She is a retired Civil Service Employee and owns a farming operation in England, Arkansas.